I want to be AN ACROBAT

Ivan Bulloch & Diane James

STARRING

LIZZIE

KATE

TOM

NICOLE

JORDAN

BECKY

MILTON

WORLD BOOK / TWO-CAN

Consultant Katie Sarabia
Photographs © Fiona Pragoff
Illustrations Derek Mathews
Design Assitant Peter Clayman

Published in the United States by
World Book, Inc.
525 W. Monroe Street
Chicago, IL
60661
in association with Two-Can Publishing Ltd.

For information on other World Book products, call 1-800-255-1750, x 2238.

Library of Congress Cataloging-in-Publication Data

Bulloch, Ivan.
    I want to be an acrobat / Ivan Bulloch & Diane James :
[photographs, Fiona Pragoff; illustrations, Derek Mathews].
        p.   cm
    "Published ... in association with Two-Can Publishing Ltd." —T.p. verso.
Includes index.
    Summary: An illustrated guide to performing basic acrobatic routines.
    ISBN 0-7166-4304-9 (hardcover). — ISBN 0-7166-4305-7 (softcover)
    1. Acrobatics—Juvenile literature. 2. Acrobats—Juvenile literature.
[1. Acrobatics.] I. James, Diane. II. Pragoff, Fiona, ill. III. Mathews, Derek, ill.
IV.Title.
GV552.B85   1997
796.47—dc21   95-50443

Printed in Hong Kong

2 3 4 5 6 7 8 9 10 01 00 99 98

CONTENTS

I WANT TO BE AN ACROBAT

You are in for a lot of hard work — but don't be put off! Spend some time on warm-up exercises and then start putting different movements together. Work on routines that you can use in a show to entertain your friends. These could be a mix of jumps, tumbles, cartwheels, and balances. The more variety you get into your act, the better.

Keep smiling, even if you are doing something really complicated.

Make sure the beginning and end of a movement look clean and neat — no wobbling!

4

Choose a partner the same size as you and try a double tumble.

A few simple props are useful. Look for plastic or wooden hoops and a good jump rope.

Always practice and perform in a safe place. You should have plenty of space. Use mats whenever possible.

Don't be afraid to ask a friend or an adult for help when you are trying something new.

LOOSEN UP!

Before you do any acrobatic routines you should do some warm-up exercises first.

Head up

When you are standing still, keep your head up, shoulders back, and your back straight. This will come naturally after a while.

Look at me!

Head up

Shoulders back

Stomach and bottom tucked in

This is ALL wrong!

Wear clothes that let you move freely.

Get those hips going!

Getting going

A hoop or jump rope is good for beginning your warm-up routine. Some background music may help to get a rhythm going. Don't spend too much time on one exercise. You need to loosen up every part of your body!

Super stretch

This is a good exercise for your hips. Squat down with your back straight and head up. Stretch each leg out to one side in turn.

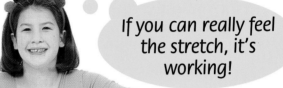

If you can really feel the stretch, it's working!

Your knee should be pointing in the same direction as your toes.

Your knee should be positioned in line with your toes.

Windmills

Swing your arms in wide circles, forward and backward. Your arms should swing close to your ears. This exercise will help loosen up your shoulders.

Keep it interesting by including some hops and jumps.

Keep your head up.

Running in place

Gently jogging in place will soon make you feel warm all over. A few minutes should be enough before moving on to another exercise.

I'm ready for the real action now!

UP IN THE AIR

How high can you jump? And how far? Try making up your own jumps by altering the position of your arms and legs in midair.

Thinking of different jumps for a routine shouldn't be a problem. There are so many to choose from. You can leap from one foot to another, jump from two feet to two feet, or from one foot to two feet. Or you can hop from one foot to the same foot! Try putting different combinations together in a routine.

TIPS

★ You can do some jumps from a standing position. Others will need a running start to give more height.
★ A perfect jump includes a safe landing. Land on the balls of your feet, then the heels, with knees and hips slightly bent.

There seems to be an awful lot to remember!

Head up, shoulders back, arms level with ears!

Try to smile, even if you are doing something really tricky.

Stretch every part of your body, and keep your arms and legs as wide as possible.

Star jump
This is an upward jump with arms and legs stretched wide. Start from a standing position and jump as high as you can!

Leapfrog

Have you ever played leapfrog? Here's a way you can play it in your act to get a good laugh! The leaper runs up as if to leap over the "frog" who is bending down. But the "frog" is not as low as usual.

It feels like flying!

I know something she doesn't!

Think up different jumps, leaps, and hops to use later in your show.

Arms stretched wide

Legs straight and toes pointed

Perform this trick only when both people know exactly what is happening.

As the leaper jumps, the "frog" catches the leaper's legs and runs off with her piggyback!

Twist and turn

You'll need to jump high for this one! Once you are airborne, turn full circle so that you land facing the direction from which you started.

UP AND OVER

Acrobats often use props in their acts. For example, a jump rope is useful and inexpensive! Another handy item is a large wooden or plastic hoop. Start jumping!

Once you have mastered plain jumping you can try some tricks. Try jumping with a partner using just one rope, or turning your rope at double speed so that it makes two turns for every jump. Instead of jumping in the same position, try moving around.

Split jump
As your rope reaches its highest point, do your best split jump. Keep one leg stretched out in front and the other leg back. Make sure the rope clears both legs!

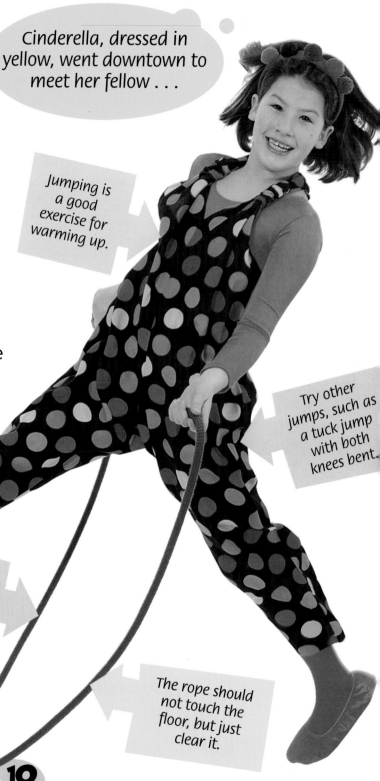

Cinderella, dressed in yellow, went downtown to meet her fellow . . .

Jumping is a good exercise for warming up.

Try other jumps, such as a tuck jump with both knees bent.

Your jump rope should not be too long!

The rope should not touch the floor, but just clear it.

Double jumping

You will need a partner to do this. Stand facing him with your rope behind you and toes nearly touching. As you jump, your partner should mirror your movements.

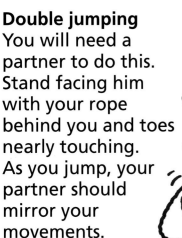

Leg pull

Here's another good use for a jump rope. Fold your rope in half and then in half again. Place your foot in the rope and raise your leg. Stretch your leg as far as you can without losing your balance.

Hoopla

Grip the hoop lightly on the top with two hands. Now start jumping in place. When you have mastered this on your own, try doing it with a partner.

ANIMAL ANTICS

Have you ever noticed what good acrobats animals are? They can jump and tumble, swing through tree branches, and do handstands and somersaults.

Watch the way an animal moves. Does it walk on all fours or on its hind legs? Which legs move at the same time? When it jumps does it take off from all four legs or just two? Now try moving like this animal. It won't be as easy as it looks!

High jump
Frogs leap high in the air using their powerful hind legs. They start from a crouched position. As they leap, their hind legs straighten and trail behind. Try it!

I don't expect I'll ever be able to jump as high as a frog!

Elephant walk
Elephants walk slowly on their heavy legs. Unlike some other four-legged animals, they move the legs on the same side of their body at the same time.

This is really hard. I don't think I've got it quite right yet!

After lift-off let your legs trail behind you.

For your show you could dress up as the animals you are pretending to be.

Crooked crab

To make yourself look like a crab, lie on your back. Push up with your hands and legs to make a strong back arch. Now try walking sideways like a crab!

Seal slither

Seals waddle around in an awkward way when they are on land, using their small flippers to push them along. (When they are swimming in the sea it's a different matter!) Try moving like a seal on land. Use your arms to propel yourself forward, letting your legs trail straight out behind you. Turn your hands out like flippers.

ROLL OVER

There are as many different rolls or tumbles as there are jumps. They can be performed slowly or at high speed.

Eyes front, palms flat!
To do a forward tumble, reach forward and take the weight of your body on your hands. Lift your bottom in the air, tuck in your head, and push off with your feet. When you are an expert tumbler you can try the hula-hoop routine with a friend.

I definitely have the easy part!

Land near in a sitting kneeling, or standing position.

Start with the hoop on the ground and gradually lift it higher.

Practice your tumbles on a soft surface!

Legs straight and arms bent

Start in a crouching position.

Your neck and the back of your head — not the top of your head — should touch the floor.

Double trouble!

It's difficult to stop this exciting double roll once it starts! One person lies on the floor with knees bent. The other person leans over and grasps his ankles. As the standing person rolls forward, the person on the ground grasps his ankles and joins in the forward roll. Both people need to work hard all the time. Even when you are the person on the floor you must be in control. This is a great act for a show.

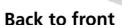

Try making different shapes with your legs in midtumble.

Try to find a partner who is the same height and build as you.

Back to front

Once you have mastered the forward roll, you shouldn't have too much trouble performing a backward roll. Start in a sitting position, arms outstretched and fingers pointing forward. Roll back and push up with your hands. Lift your hips high in the air.

UPSIDE-DOWN WORLD!

Try a headstand or a handstand and you'll get a different view of things!

Legs straight and stretched out wide, toes pointed

Try bringing your feet back together again from this position.

I'm just as happy on my head as on my feet!

Head down

When you try a headstand for the first time it's a good idea to have a friend to help you. The friend can help support your back until you can balance on your own.

Use a mat or a cushion to start with.

If you can't find a friend, use the wall instead!

Take the weight on your forehead, not the top of your head.

Take off with one foot and bring the other one up to join it. Try a basic headstand with legs and body straight before you go on to make different shapes.

When you are confident at balancing in a handstand position, you can try walking on your hands.

Hand, hand, foot, foot

Once you've mastered headstands and handstands, cartwheels will be easy. Your leading hand should hit the floor first, followed by your other hand and then each foot in turn. Try to keep your legs straight.

This is a speedy way to get from one place to another.

Hands down

A good way to start practicing handstands is against a wall. This will keep your legs from going over and help you balance. Try to get your body as straight as possible. Avoid curving your back. A friend can tell you how your form looks.

KEEP STEADY!

Some people find it easier to balance than others. But if you practice hard you'll be able to do it. Remember when you started to ride a bike or had on your first pair of rollerskates?

Tin-can stilts

You have probably seen performers using tall wooden stilts, but these stilts are easy to make and good for beginners!

Look for two cans the same size. Large coffee cans are ideal. Ask an adult to punch holes on either side at the bottom. Thread a piece of string through each hole and knot it under the can.

It's great being so tall!

Keep the string taut and lift each can in turn.

The string should be long enough for you to grip when your arms are straight.

Decorate your stilts with paint or colored paper.

Tightrope walking

If you've ever seen a circus you were probably amazed by the daring skills of acrobats balancing on a wire high above the ring. Try it out for yourself, but closer to the ground! A long, low bench is good to start with. Keep your head up, body straight, and toes pointed.

Tightrope walkers often use a pole to help them balance. An umbrella may help, too.

Holding your arms out to the side will help you keep your balance

Hold still

You can balance all sorts of things on different parts of your body. Try a giant feather on the end of your nose or the end of a broom or a tennis racket on the palm of your hand.

DOUBLE ACT

Working with a partner will allow you to do things that you can't do on your own.

King of the castle
Take this balance slowly and carefully! The person kneeling on all fours must keep his back completely straight.

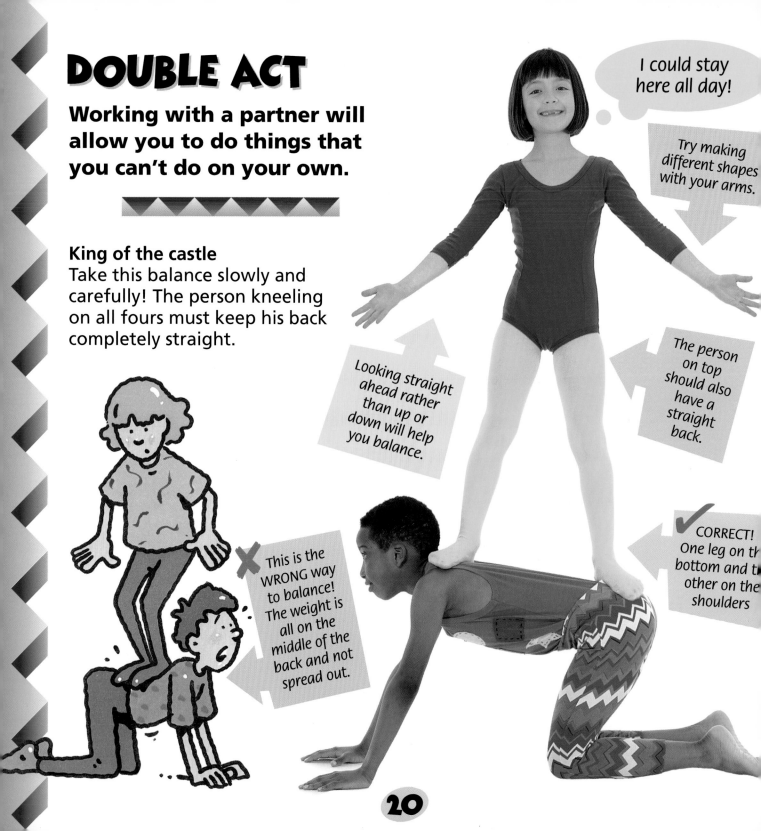

I could stay here all day!

Try making different shapes with your arms.

Looking straight ahead rather than up or down will help you balance.

The person on top should also have a straight back.

This is the WRONG way to balance! The weight is all on the middle of the back and not spread out.

✓ CORRECT! One leg on th bottom and t other on the shoulders

Back to back

Here's another balancing act to try with a friend. One person kneels on all fours as before. The person going on top stands with her back to his, legs astride his. Then she sits down gently on the other person's bottom, slowly leaning back until she is lying down.

Look! We're balancing each other.

I hope he doesn't let go!

Don't let go!

This balancing act is known as a counterbalance. Both partners are balancing each other. It is very important that the arms are straight, knees bent, and toes touching. Use the grip shown in the picture. It will keep your hands from slipping.

Knees bent

Toes touching

21

HOW LOW CAN YOU GO?

This is a great act to try when you are feeling in terrific shape and your body is really supple.

Hmm! It looks kind of low to me, but I'll try!

Take your hat off before it falls off.

Let's limbo

The limbo is an acrobatic dance that comes from the West Indies. A pole is set up between two posts. It starts about chest-high. Performers bend their knees and shuffle forward under the pole. This is easy when the pole is high, but after each turn it gets lower and lower!

Hips pushed forward

If the pole is very low, tip your head back at the last minute.

Knees bent and wide apart

Feet flat on floor

Make your own

If you want to try the limbo, you'll need a set of posts and a long pole. Don't forget that you will have to raise and lower the pole. Cut two side posts exactly the same from thick corrugated cardboard. Make slits at the top and bottom of each. Then cut notches at equal distances along one side of each post. These are for the pole to rest on. Use a long broom handle or a dowel rod for the pole.

I don't think I have the hang of this!

Don't make this too heavy in case it falls on top of you!

Paint all the pieces in bright colors before you assemble them.

Make two of these triangular pieces to slot into the side posts. They will make the posts stand up on their own.

Make two of these semi-circles to slot into the tops of the side posts. They are only for decoration!

Beat the record

If you want to be a world-champion limbo dancer, you'll have to practice hard! The best limbo dancers can shuffle and wiggle under a post that is only about 6 inches high!

23

ONE, TWO, THREE!

The most important requirement for these balancing acts is that you have three or more people. It helps if everyone is roughly the same size.

Caterpillar crawl

To start, sit in a line in front of one another with legs apart and arms out to the side. Then everyone gently rocks from side to side.

At the same time, everyone swings to one side, lifting one leg then the other over the person in front so that they all end up facing the floor. Each bends his knees and tucks his feet up. Now the caterpillar can move slowly forward!

It may help to count out loud – 1, 2, 3, and over!

To break the caterpillar up, each person rolls forward in turn, starting with the person at the front.

Don't hold the position for too long — just long enough for your audience to admire it.

Three's company, too!

Practice different balancing shapes with three people. You can work out a routine which includes different shapes. Try to move from one to the next smoothly. Don't try to be too fancy or attempt anything dangerous! You can see from the ideas here that even simple balances look good. When you are practicing, have a friend stand by to help.

The person on the bottom should have a straight back.

Break your balances down as neatly as possible when they are finished.

I don't feel like a caterpillar — more like the monkey in the middle!

Heads up and big smiles, even if the person on top weighs a ton!

JUMP, TUMBLE, TWIST!

Juggling with people is kind of like juggling with balls. Once you are used to the rhythm, it's easy! The routine includes jumps and forward tumbles.

Give each person a letter so that he knows what he is doing! The movement starts with the illustration below. **A** and **B** stand facing each other with **C** in the middle facing **A**. **C** does a forward roll toward **A**. **A** jumps over **C**.

It may help to practice this with music in the background to get a rhythm going.

Practice jumps and tumbles on your own before trying this one.

Here I go again!

In the photograph, **C** has finished the roll, jumped up, and is twisting around to face the middle again. **A** does a forward roll toward **B** and **B** jumps over.

In the illustration above, **A** has finished the roll, jumped up, and twisted round to face the middle again. **B** is doing a forward roll toward **C**. **C** jumps over **B**. The pattern continues in the same way until everyone is exhausted! This routine would make a good finale for your show. But make sure that the act before is not too energetic!

BEFORE THE SHOW

By now you will be in great shape and nearly ready to put on a show for your friends. There are quite a few things to think about before the big day arrives.

Rehearsals

Practice your routines until you feel really confident. The day before your show, have a run-through with costumes and props.

Spreading the word

Make sure all your friends and family know about your show in plenty of time. Make invitations and posters with an acrobatic theme.

Make a bear mask to go with a funny bear walk!

Set up all your props in plenty of time.

Make sure your costume is comfortable.

Dressing up

Acrobats usually wear close-fitting clothes, such as tights, leotards, and and leggings. This makes it easier to see the amazing shapes they make with their bodies.

Won't you get tangled in that?

I'm getting butterflies in my stomach but I'm sure it will be fine on the day.

The day before the show, have a full dress rehearsal and time the program.

If everything is well-planned and rehearsed, you are less likely to panic on the day of the show.

The show

Your show doesn't need to be long, but it should be well planned. You may decide to work to a theme or to put together a series of different acts. Whatever you decide, try to vary the pace within the show so that it is not all fast and furious.

SHOW TIME

The big day has arrived and it's time for the show! You have been rehearsing until your act is perfect and now you are going to try it out in front of a real, live audience. There's no time to feel nervous. The show must go on!

Ladies and gentlemen, please give a big hand to Jumping Jordan and Tumbling Tom!

The presenter can also take part in the show.

MAKE SURE YOU ALLOW AT LEAST HALF AN HOUR BEFORE THE SHOW FOR A GOOD WARM-UP SESSION.

★

CHECK THROUGH ALL YOUR PROPS BEFORE THE SHOW.

★

INCLUDE AS MANY DIFFERENT MOVEMENTS AND ROUTINES AS POSSIBLE TO MAKE YOUR ACT EXCITING.

★

IF SOMETHING GOES WRONG, JUST CARRY ON!

You can make your routines more fun by doing some acting at the same time as showing off your acrobatic skills. What's happened here is that the waiter – on all fours – has dropped his tray and bent down to pick everything up. His friend has popped in to visit! Seeing him bent over on the floor, he decided to play a trick and quickly climbed onto his back without being noticed!

INDEX

Hope you had as much fun as we did!